Creativity

Ready, Steady, Play!

Series Editor: Sandy Green

Guaranteed fun for children and practitioners alike, the Ready, Steady, Play! series provides lively and stimulating activities for children.

Each book focuses on one specific aspect of play offering clear and detailed guidance on how to plan and enjoy wonderful play experiences with minimum fuss and maximum success.

Each book in the Ready, Steady, Play! series includes advice on:

- How to prepare the children and the play space
- What equipment and materials are needed
- How much time is needed to prepare and carry out the activity
- How many staff are required
- How to communicate with parents and colleagues

Ready, Steady, Play! helps you to:

- Develop activities easily, using suggested guidelines
- Ensure that health and safety issues are taken into account
- Plan play that links to the early years curriculum
- Broaden your understanding of early years issues

Early years practitioners and students on early years courses and parents looking for simple, excellent ideas for creative play will love these books!

Other titles in the series

Books, Stories and Puppets 1-84312-148-4 Green
Construction 1-84312-098-4 Boyd
Displays and Interest Tables 1-84312-267-7 Olpin
Festivals 1-84312-101-8 Hewitson
Food and Cooking 1-84312-100-X Green
Music and Singing 1-84312-276-6 Green
Nature, Living and Growing 1-84312-114-X Harper
Play Using Natural Materials 1-84312-099-2 Howe
Role Play 1-84312-147-6 Green

372.21
G82

Creativity

Sandy Green

Nyack College Library

 David Fulton Publishers

David Fulton Publishers Ltd
The Chiswick Centre, 414 Chiswick High Road, London W4 5TF

www.fultonpublishers.co.uk

First published in Great Britain in 2004 by David Fulton Publishers

10 9 8 7 6 5 4 3 2 1

Note: The right of Sandy Green to be identified as the author of this work has been asserted by her in accordance with the Copyright, Designs and Patents Act 1988.

David Fulton Publishers is a division of Granada Learning Limited, part of ITV plc.

Copyright © Sandy Green 2004

British Library Cataloguing in Publication Data
A catalogue record for this book is available from the British Library.

ISBN 1-84312-076-3

The materials in this publication may be photocopied only for use within the purchasing organisation. Otherwise, all rights reserved. No part of this publication may be reproduced, stored in a retrieval system or transmitted, in any form or by any means, electronic, mechanical, photocopying, or otherwise, without the prior permission of the publishers.

Typeset by FiSH Books, London
Printed and bound in Great Britain

#5646634

Contents

Creativity

Welcome to *Creativity*, an exciting new publication which is part of the Ready, Steady, Play! series.

Get ready to enjoy a range of activities with your children, which will stimulate their all-round development.

The Ready, Steady, Play! books will help boost the confidence of new practitioners by providing informative and fun ideas to support planning and preparation. The series will also consolidate and extend learning for the more experienced practitioner. Attention is drawn to health and safety, and the role of the adult is addressed.

Acknowledgements

Thanks are due to my husband John for his ongoing support and to Nina Stibbe at David Fulton Publishers for her tireless enthusiasm. Thanks, also, to GALT for permission to use their pictures.

Series acknowledgement

The series editor would like to thank the children, parents and staff at:

The Nursery and Reception classes at Wadebridge Community Primary School, Wadebridge, Cornwall
Happy Days Day Nursery, Wadebridge, Cornwall
Snapdragons Nursery, Weston, Bath, Somerset
Snapdragons Nursery, Grosvenor, Bath, Somerset
Tadpoles Nursery, Combe Down, Bath, Somerset

for letting us take photographs of their excellent provision, resources and displays.

Thanks, also, to John and Jake Green, Hannah, Alan and Jazzy Beech for help taking and agreeing to photographs, and to Paul Isbell at David Fulton Publishers for his patience, enthusiasm and support throughout the series.

Introduction

In the provision of creative activities within early years settings, children are given opportunities for expression, communication and exploration. It is important that as practitioners we enable children to work as freely with the materials provided as is possible, since too much adult direction will lessen much of the scope for these vital aspects of learning.

Creativity is an important part of the early years curriculum. Being creative means bringing something of yourself to all that you do. Creativity as an area of learning includes painting, drawing and colouring, collage, printing and junk modelling, weaving, sewing and malleable play, producing creative items in both two and three dimensions. Music-making and appreciation, and drama also form part of the creative curriculum. These aspects are covered elsewhere in the Ready, Steady, Play! Series, in *Music and Singing* and *Role Play*.

Creative outcomes are very personal to each individual child, as they will always have something of themselves within each creation. It is important that as adult professionals we value and show appreciation of the effort a child has put in. This can be achieved through praise and encouragement, both during and after the activity has been completed, and by displaying their work appropriately (see pages 9, 55, 73).

How to use this book

Creativity is divided into three main sections. The first section provides a range of information for practitioners and discussion pages for use with children, perhaps during a group time, or preceding some of the activities. The playdough recipes provide a range of alternatives, depending on the type of play experience desired. There is also a recipe for gluten-free playdough which will be useful for any setting with a child attending who has the condition coeliac, meaning they are sensitive to the protein gluten, found in wheat, barley, oats and rye.

The stages of drawing on page 6 show the usual process of mark-making development, and will, I am sure, be of interest to all practitioners. This shows clearly how the drawing process develops, and observation will confirm how all children go through a similar set of stages.

The second section of this book provides a range of activities that can be enjoyed with young children. Most of these involve the use of paint, glue and other 'creative' materials. The section is preceded by guidance on basic creative skills and on making different paints, use of utensils and so on. Each activity provides guidance as to resources, aims and process, and gives practical advice on adult:child ratios, health and safety points, and ways of extending the activity further. The suggested vocabulary and discussion ideas are exactly that – suggestions. They should not be seen as prescriptive or comprehensive. They are given to guide new and less experienced practitioners in how to introduce and enhance language use through practical situations, and to prompt and consolidate language use for more experienced practitioners.

The final section provides a range of photocopiable sheets which children will enjoy exploring. These are mostly linked to colour use and recognition. They will enhance learning further in a fun and informative way.

Providing creative opportunities for children as part of the day-to-day curriculum provides them with the following key learning opportunities:

- the opportunity to express themselves;
- the opportunity to communicate through non-verbal means;
- the opportunity to explore a range of media;
- the development of fine motor skills;
- language development through discussion and questioning as an individual, one to one with an adult, or within a group situation;
- concentration skills, as they focus on each aspect of what they are doing;
- emotional satisfaction regarding effort and achievement;
- exploration and investigative opportunities.

Health and safety

Health and safety during creative activities must never be ignored. Relevant points have been indicated for each of the activities in this book. They include:

- Appropriate adult:child ratios always being in place.
- Limited numbers particularly when closer supervision is needed (e.g. when sewing).
- Adult supervision being essential when resources such as scissors, glues and staplers are being used.
- Remembering that creative activities produce 'mess' and they therefore need to be situated away from other activities, allowing more freedom for the children and less concern for the impact on other activity areas.
- All materials used being non-toxic, and items such as 'lolly' sticks should be obtained from craft suppliers rather than gathered from any other means.
- Cleaning materials also being non-toxic, and kept out of reach of young children.

- Practitioners ensuring that any allergies, such as to cotton wool, are taken into account, and that alternative resources are provided for the children affected.
- Hand-washing facilities needing to be close by to avoid unnecessary dripping of paint, and therefore slippery floor surfaces.
- Practitioners ensuring that children follow all basic health and safety rules such as not walking around carrying scissors.
- All resources being stored safely.

The adult role

As well as ensuring a healthy and safe environment for the children during creative activities, the adult has a number of other important roles. These include:

- Planning activities carefully, ensuring an anti-discriminatory approach is taken at all times.
- Providing appropriate tools and resources for each activity.
- Providing sufficient tools and resources for each activity.
- Giving praise and encouragement.
- Supporting learning through challenge and stimulation.
- Encouraging language use and vocabulary extension through discussion and open questioning.
- Observing children and assessing their progress.
- Providing extension activities where appropriate.

Stages of early drawing

Children are ready to draw as soon as they have mastered the skill of holding a crayon. This is the ideal time to introduce paper and mark-making to them. Their initial marks will most likely be from side to side in just one direction, gradually increasing in skill to movements in more than one direction, necessitating lifting the crayon from the paper and repositioning it. The third stage will be to draw circle-type shapes, the beginnings of the outlines needed for people and other lifelike replications.

The development of drawing is a gradual process, evolving over a considerable length of time. It is a skill that needs practice, and children will benefit from opportunities to enjoy a range of different mark-making activities, trying a range of different media and handling a variety of implements.

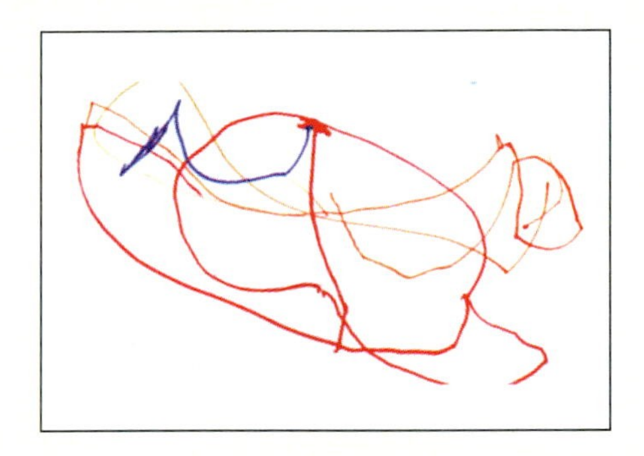

Children sometimes use drawing to express their feelings and to demonstrate elements of their experiences. They will often draw aspects of what they have seen, or of important events in their lives. The most important aspects of their pictures are usually the most prominent.

At times children will cover up a 'super' picture with paint or 'scribble'. Adults are often disappointed to see a 'masterpiece' disappear in this way. However, from the children's point of view it often means that they have finished the picture. It is of no further use for them, in much the same way as a model made from playdough is finished with, being proudly displayed one minute and squashed flat the next.

The 13 main stages of early drawing are listed below. No age should be attached to each stage, as all children will develop at their own pace, with most stages following on in a similar order.

Stage one

Stage two

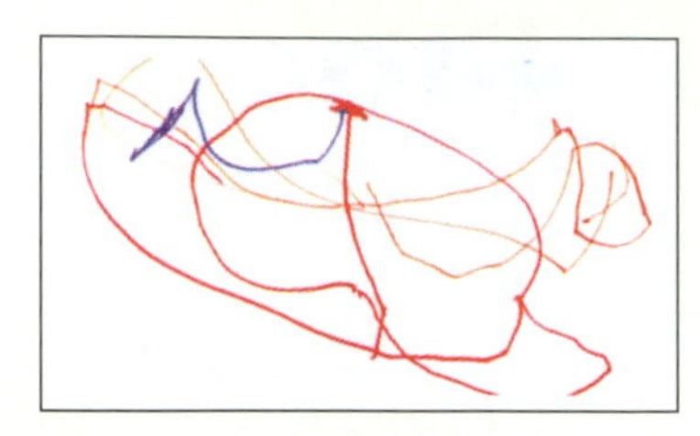

Stage three

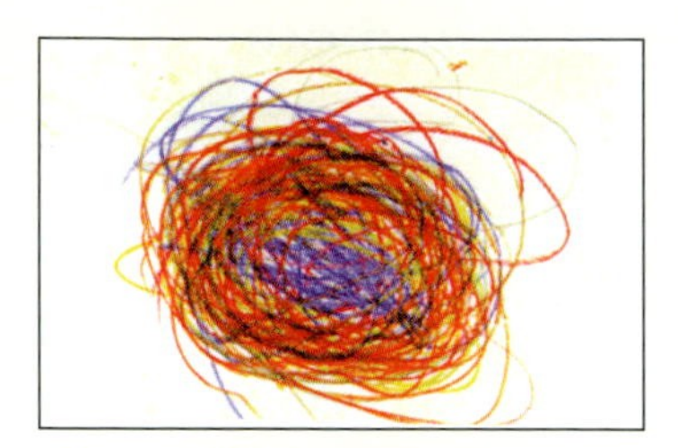

Stage four

Stage five

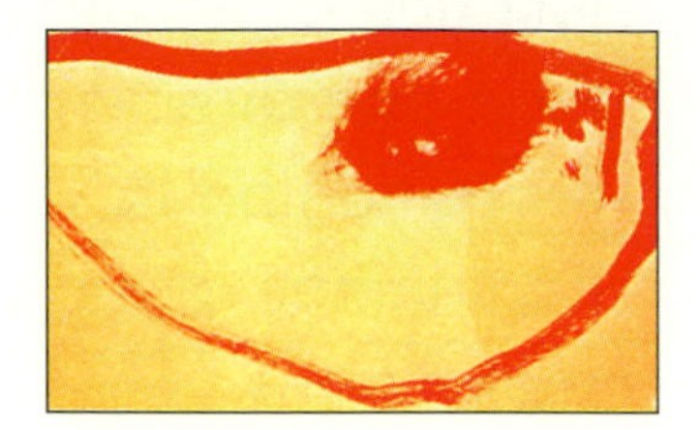

Stage six

Stage seven

Stage eight

Stage nine

Stage ten

Stage eleven

Stage twelve

Stage thirteen

Preparing the environment

Creativity will undoubtedly bring mess. This should not be a problem so long as the environment is prepared in advance.

The first aspect to consider is the positioning of creative play. Think through the following:

- What activities are nearby? Will they be adversely affected?
- Does the work surface to be used need covering? Usually newspaper or a wipe-clean cloth works best.
- Should the floor be covered? This will depend on the extent to which you think 'creativity' will travel. It is a must for finger painting and similar expressiveness. Again, newspaper is ideal.
- What about hand-washing? Is there a child-height sink nearby? If not, should a bowl be positioned nearby to 'take off the worst'? Children can then go and wash properly in the usual way.

Once creativity has taken place, it will be necessary to dry any 'masterpieces'. Again, you need to think about where this will happen. An old clothes horse will suffice for paintings on large sheets if you do not have a painting stacker, but a table, cupboard top or shelf will be needed to dry smaller sheets or 3D models.

Displaying creativity appropriately

All children deserve to have their creations treated with respect. This places value on what they do and helps to raise self-esteem.

It is important that displays include the work of every child at some time, not only the most creatively advanced. A display of children's 'work' should be what it says – products of the children. It should not be a display of adult-directed and 'accurate' pictures.

Even the most abstract daub can look effective when mounted carefully.

Mounting pictures should not be rushed. They look best when set against a contrasting background sheet, leaving a slightly larger gap at the bottom than at the top.

Covering a display board with a background colour always shows off display work at its best. If you can afford it, a display border can give a very professional finish.

Remember

At times a child may use only a small area of the paper for a picture, but this does not mean that you should ignore the 'waste' and display only the drawing. The context of 'image within space' may have a particular meaning for the child.

Paint

Providing paint

It is easy to make up the same colour paint week in, week out. Many settings use primary colours as a matter of course. Try to ring the changes by using more unusual shades such as turquoise, magenta or primrose. Add white to provide pale colours, or provide four different shades of the same colour. Listen to children's comments on these changes, and explore their thoughts with them.

Making up paint

Before making up paint for an activity, you first need to decide what you are aiming the children to experience and do with it. The consistency of paint is important, and can be vital to the success of the overall activity. Paint that is too thin and runny will not be successful when finger painting. Conversely, paint that is too thick will not be suitable for blow painting. The following guidelines provide a useful point of reference when preparing your materials.

Paint can be made up using powder and water, or it can be purchased ready-made. The latter is often more convenient, but is also more expensive. Whenever practical, make up the paint with the children. This gives them vital experience regarding the combining of materials, and helps them to understand how different types of paint effects can be achieved.

Children enjoy the science of making up paint, watching it move from the powdered state to the smooth, creamy mixture that they work with. There is also much to be gained by letting children mix their own colours, either freely, or to achieve a planned outcome, perhaps supporting a specific aspect of learning. Try providing a range of other 'ingredients' for paint-making too (see page 74).

The use of pots with non-spill lids is ideal for younger children. Using old plates or shallow dishes lined with thin sponge or kitchen paper can be useful for printing. For the more adventurous practitioners, washing-up liquid bottles provide a wonderful experience, but are best used out of doors and away from other activities!

Thin paint

Make up fairly watery paint and add a small amount of washing-up liquid. This is ideal for bubble painting (see page 52).

Medium thickness paint

A generous amount of powder paint to water is needed to obtain strength of colour. Add a small amount of powder paste to thicken it slightly. Washing-up liquid can also be used as a thickener. It helps it wash out, too! This paint is suitable for straightforward easel painting and printing.

Thickened paint

Make paint thick enough so that it does not drip by adding soap flakes, flour or powder paste. Add it in stages over a period of a few minutes, as the paint will thicken gradually.

This paint is ideal for:

- printing in general (see pages 48, 60)
- string painting (see page 50)

- hand printing (see page 60)
- foot printing (see page 62)
- painting junk models (see page 46)
- butterfly prints (see page 54)

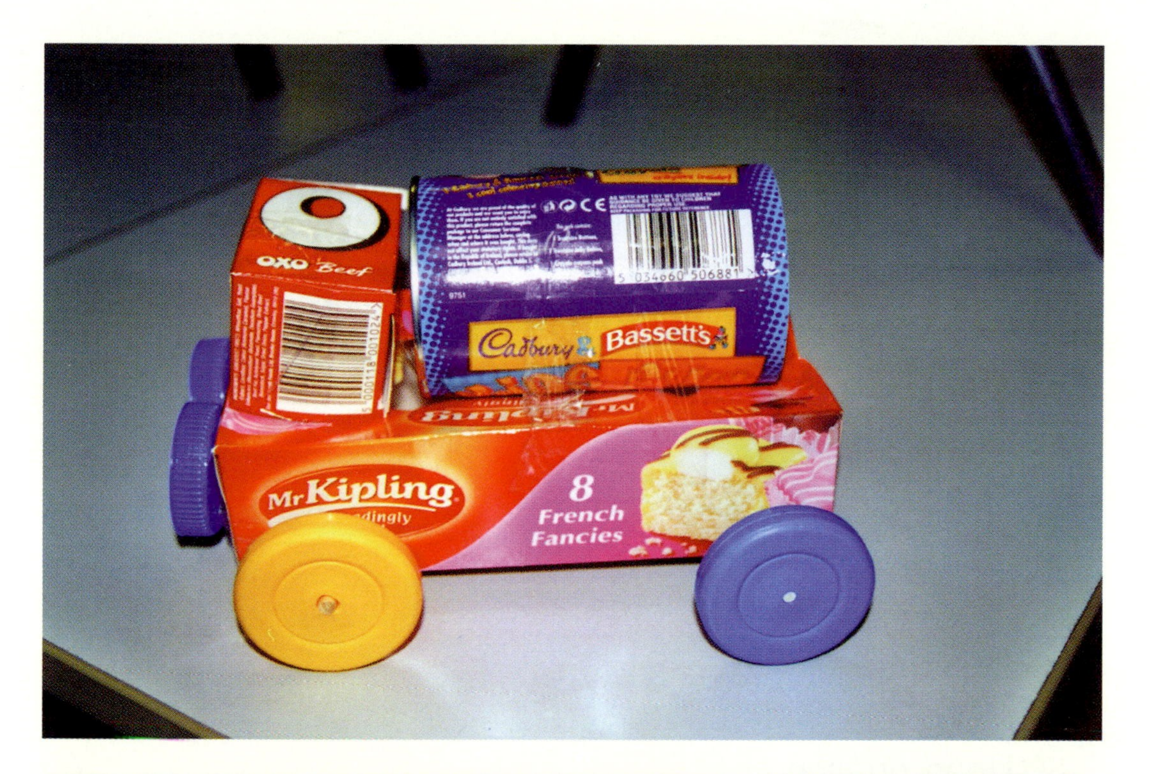

An 'at-a-glance' chart to providing the ideal paint

Key: Thin paint

Medium paint

Thick paint

Icon	Activities that work best	page
Thin	Bubble painting	52
	Wax paintings	58
Medium	Mehndi painting	30
	Making a honeycomb from hexagons	34
	Making wrapping paper	36
	Three-dimensional flying insects	42
	Self-portraits	44
	Printing	48
	Butterfly prints	54
	Using patchwork designs	68
Thick	Model-making with junk	46
	String painting	50
	Hand printing	60
	Foot printing	62
	Finger painting	66

Finger painting

Mixture 1

Mix equal parts of powder paint and washing-up liquid. Provide two or three colours. Let each child choose two colours and put a spoonful of each on to a washable surface.

Encourage them to swirl the paint about with their hands and fingers.

Mixture 2

Using a hand whisk (or, better, an electric mixer), beat around 250ml of washing-up liquid to a thick froth. It will resemble whisked egg-whites. Place a large dollop of the mixture in front of each child and help them sprinkle powder paint over the froth. The children will enjoy turning the froth from white to their chosen colour, again using hands and fingers.

Mixture 3

Place 2 cups of flour and 5 cups of cold water in a saucepan. Cook gently until smooth, then add 1 teaspoon of salt. Leave to cool and then add colouring. NB: This paint is not suitable for children with the gluten intolerance condition coeliac.

Refer also to finger-painting activity on page 66.

'Magic' paint mixtures

Icing sugar painting

Mix up a watery solution of icing sugar and water.

Encourage the children to paint with this solution on strong, non-absorbent paper, then provide sprinklers (see page 17) of powder paint to shake over the mixture. Let them enjoy seeing how the patterns spread.

This mixture takes a while to dry, and has a lovely shiny finish.

Oil and water painting

Combine vegetable oil with a little powder paint to make oil paints.

Half fill a washing-up bowl with water.

Encourage the children to drop a couple of teaspoons of the oil paint on to the surface of the water and swirl it about with a craft lolly stick.

Float copier paper on the surface and see the lovely patterns that can be achieved.

Sprinkle painting

Mix together equal quantities of powder paint and salt (or white sand).

Encourage the children to paint the surface of their paper with glue or a made-up paste. Let them see the effect when they sprinkle the powder mixture over the sticky surface.

Brushes, utensils and surfaces

Whenever possible, provide a whole range of brushes and utensils for the children to choose from. Display these so that children can select which to use. These may include:

- long-handled thin brushes
- long-handled fat brushes
- short-handled thin brushes
- short-handled fat brushes
- household paintbrushes
- stencil brushes
- toothbrushes
- shaving brushes
- clean plastic roll-on deodorant bottles (great for little hands and those with limited dexterity)
- decorator's rollers – with thick string or rubber bands around the metal frame
- large pepper or flour shakers for sprinkling on powder paint.

Depending on the activity you are setting up, provide items for printing with and pulling through paint, such as:

- sponges
- combs
- cotton reels – end on for circle patterns, sideways for 'tracks'
- string (see page 50)
- corks
- leaves
- yoghurt pots
- smoothed-off ends of woodblocks
- cream cartons – cut down the sides in strips and use as a 'stamp' – very messy, but great fun
- fruit and vegetables (see page 48)
- old biscuit cutters.

NB: Rollers, stamps and print blocks can also be commercially bought.

Remember

Although it is generally believed that younger children will cope best with shorter brushes, it is important that they are given a range of opportunities to try other implements. This will help them develop physically and spatially, and add to their creative development.

Surfaces to paint on

Whenever possible, give children large sheets of paper – A3 is good, A2 is much better. This allows for the larger arm use of younger children and decreases the restrictions on the flow of their painting.

When encouraging foot printing (see page 62), use rolls of lining paper or old wallpaper – let the children walk while they print. This is much more fun than simply taking a print!

Use unwanted lengths of plain sheeting, and make your own design drapes and curtains for the role-play area, or use as a background for other display work.

Think about the suitability of the paper you are providing. Ask yourself:

- Is it strong enough for the activity or is it likely to tear?
- Is it large enough to allow freedom of expression?
- Is it absorbent enough for the planned activity?
- Will it let the paint flow, if required by the activity?
- Would white paper be better than coloured paper?

Playdough

Playing with playdough is an activity enjoyed by most young children. It should ideally be offered as an unstructured, freeplay activity without adult direction.

Practitioners often seem to put out a range of tools with playdough as a matter of course, but sometimes we should encourage children simply to handle the dough, helping them to engage directly with it, before providing cutters, rolling-pins and so on which automatically remove direct contact with the dough.

The role of the adult at the dough table is to discuss with the children what they are doing, encouraging vocabulary which describes their experience (e.g. mould, shape, squeeze).

On occasions, practitioners can enhance the children's experience by mixing items such as glittery stars or jumbo oats into the dough. This gives alternative visual and tactile stimulation. Food essence such as lemon can stimulate their olfactory senses too.

It should be remembered that the inclusion of oats is not appropriate in gluten-free playdough (see page 23), as many children with the gluten intolerance condition coeliac have an intolerance to oats too.

Making playdough – cooked recipe

Cooked playdough probably lasts longer than any other type of dough. However, it should be replaced regularly, particularly if a viral infection has entered the setting.

Ingredients

2 cups flour
1 cup salt
2 cups water
2 tablespoons cooking oil (sunflower or vegetable)
2 teaspoons cream of tartar
1 teaspoon food colouring (optional)

Method

1. Place all the ingredients in a pan.
2. Cook over a gentle heat, stirring continuously.
3. When the dough mixture 'comes away' from the sides of the pan, it is ready.
4. Turn the dough out on to a board.
5. Knead well to remove any lumps.
6. When cool, store in an airtight container in the refrigerator.

Making playdough – uncooked recipes

Each of these recipes is ideal for when working with children (see page 70 for further details).

Recipe 1 – non-stretchy dough

Ingredients

1.5kg plain flour
500kg cooking salt
Approximately 750ml water

Method

1. Combine the flour and salt in a large bowl.
2. Gradually add the water.
3. Knead well to obtain a smooth texture.

This dough will break cleanly. It holds its shape well, and can be pulled apart into small pieces and squashed back together again. It does not stretch.

Recipe 2 – stretchy dough

Ingredients

1.5kg self-raising flour
Approximately 750ml water
No salt

Method

1. Gradually add the water to the flour.
2. Knead the dough well to obtain a very smooth consistency.

This dough is stretchy and does not break into clean 'chunks'. It can be stretched into a 'dough rope' and swung gently. If holes are poked into this type of dough, they will gradually fill up again.

Recipe 3 – super-stretchy dough

Ingredients

1.5kg strong bread flour
750ml water
No salt

Method

1. Gradually add the water to the flour.
2. Knead well to obtain a very smooth consistency.

This dough resembles strong elastic. It can be stretched into long lengths and swung like a lasso!

Making playdough – a gluten-free recipe

Children who have the condition coeliac have an intolerance to the substance gluten which is found in wheat, barley, rye and oats. For some, the effects are seen only when they have eaten something containing these foods, but for others, simply handling them can cause problems.

It is important to remember that playdough is usually made with wheat-based flour and is therefore not suitable for a child with coeliac. The following recipe offers a useful alternative that can be safely used by both coeliac and non-coeliac children.

Remember

Although adding texture to playdough can enhance the experience for the children, foods such as oats should *not* be included within this recipe.

Ingredients

1 cup rice flour
1 cup cornflour
1 cup salt
4 teaspoons cream of tartar
2 cups water
2 tablespoons vegetable oil
Food colouring (optional)

Method

1. Place all the ingredients together in a saucepan.
2. Stir well while cooking the mixture over a gentle heat.
3. Continue to stir. The mixture will change from a runny consistency to a firmer consistency.
4. Remove pan from the heat and turn the dough out on to a board.
5. Knead the dough well to achieve a smooth texture throughout.
6. When cooled, place dough in a plastic container and store in the refrigerator until required.

Playdough keeps well if refrigerated between uses, but should be regularly replaced for hygiene reasons, particularly if an infectious illness has entered the setting.

Discussing colour with children

Use the following pages to talk about colour and colour blends with children.

Discussion page

Discussion page

Discussion page

Activities

The following pages contain 24 different activities suggesting a range of different creative ideas. Each activity follows a standard format to ensure ease of planning and implementation:

- the resources needed
- the aim(s)/concept(s)
- the process
- group size
- health and safety
- vocabulary/discussion
- extension ideas
- links to the Foundation Stage Curriculum.

Key to Foundation Stage Curriculum abbreviations:

SS	Stepping Stones
ELG	Early Learning Goals
PSE	Personal, social and emotional development
CLL	Communication, language and literacy
MD	Mathematical development
KUW	Knowledge and understanding of the world
PD	Physical development
CD	Creative development

ACTIVITY 1

Taking 'rubbings'

Resources you will need

- Sheets of medium-weight paper for each child
- Colouring medium such as wax crayons, chalks, pencils
- A range of items to be rubbed, each with a raised surface texture (bark and leaves are ideal)

Aim/concept

- To help children obtain a representation through the use of texture

Process

- Explain to the children what they are going to be doing.
- Ask them for ideas of what they could use.
- If possible, take them outside to find natural items such as bark, leaves and flat stones.
- Ask them also what they can find from inside the setting.
- Give each child a sheet of paper and a suitable colouring medium.
- Show the children how to hold the paper still to achieve the best results.
- Encourage the children to experiment with as many rubbings as they wish, asking them which were most successful and why.

Vocabulary/discussion

- Name each item used
- Encourage descriptive words such as knobbly, smooth, rough, grained, layered, textured, raised
- Use words such as touch, feel, handle, caress, explore, massage, tactile, stroke

Group size

6

Links to Foundation Stage Curriculum

SS Build up vocabulary that reflects the breadth of the children's experiences (CLL)

ELG Extend their vocabulary, exploring the meanings and sounds of new words (CLL)

SS Demonstrate increasing skill and control in the use of mark-making implements, blocks, construction sets and 'small world' activities (PD)

ELG Handle tools, objects, construction and malleable materials safely and with increasing control (PD)

Extension ideas

1. Link to a topic on the natural environment (if only using bark, leaves and so on).
2. Make a display of different types of patterns.
3. Play games involving texture, such as 'What's in the feely bag?'
4. Read stories with textured pictures.
5. Make a display of items with differing textures.

Health and safety

⚠ Suitability of items used regarding sharp edges and cleanliness

ACTIVITY 2 Mehndi hand painting

Resources you will need

- Sheets of A4 paper for each child
- Containers of suitable coloured paints (black, red, blue, white)
- Pictures of decorated hands as examples

Aim/concept

- To introduce a feature of another culture, and to explore the use of colour for a purpose

Process

- Show the children the pictures of decorated (Mehndi) hand designs.
- Explain that this is a traditional activity carried out by Hindu and Muslim girls and young women at festivals and weddings.
- Talk about the colours and patterns that can be used.
- Emphasise the need for careful pattern formation.
- Show the children how to hold their hands flat down on the paper to draw around them. Adult help may be needed here, or you may choose to use the photocopiable sheet on page 82.
- Demonstrate painting slowly and carefully on your own 'hand' shape.
- Encourage the children to make their own Mehndi designs.
- Talk to the children about colour and patterns throughout the activity.

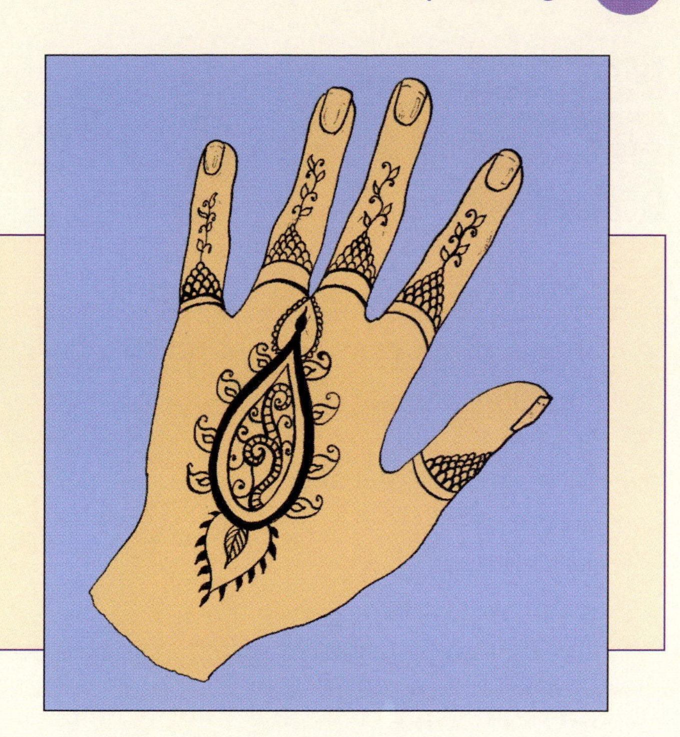

Vocabulary/discussion

- Names of colours
- Names of shapes: circles, flowers, stars, zigzags, lines, squiggles, dots
- Mehndi, Asian culture, festival, wedding

Group size

6–8

Links to Foundation Stage Curriculum

SS Have a positive approach to new experiences (PSE)

ELG Continue to be interested, excited and motivated to learn (PSE)

SS Gain an awareness of the cultures and beliefs of others (KUW)

ELG Gain a knowledge of their own cultures and beliefs and those of other people (KUW)

SS Work creatively on a large or small scale (CD)

ELG Explore colour, texture, shape, form and space in 2- or 3D (CD)

Extension ideas

1. Link to range of Asian festivals.
2. Use designs to make Divali cards (usually celebrated late October/early November).
3. Tell stories linked to Asian festivals such as Rama and Sita.
4. Explore other ways that Asian culture celebrates festivals such as:
   - Divali – Festival of Lights, using little clay lamps
   - Holi – the grand festival of colour, celebrated in spring with dancing and bonfires.

Health and safety

⚠ Use of non-toxic paints

⚠ Careful supervision of scissors use if hand shapes are to be cut out

ACTIVITY 3

A natural collage

Resources you will need

- Sheets of medium-weight paper
- PVA glue
- Spatulas
- A range of natural resources (e.g. leaves, sunflower seeds, flower heads, acorns, grass, pine needles, feathers, gravel)

Aim/concept

- To produce a textured collage using natural resources only

Process

- Show the children the range of resources you have provided for them, and ask them what they notice about them (they are all natural).
- If possible, enable the children to collect resources themselves from around the outside play area of the setting.
- Give each child a sheet of paper and a spatula.
- Encourage the children to select and create, using the resources of their choice.
- Encourage the children to feel, smell, compare and talk about the resources as they use them.

Vocabulary/discussion

- Names of the natural resource items, colour names, shapes, where items are found, where else seen, times of year (e.g. spring, autumn)
- Discuss the resources, using all the appropriate senses
- Encourage the children to describe what they are seeing, feeling and smelling

Group size

4–6

Links to Foundation Stage Curriculum

SS Build up vocabulary that reflects the breadth of their experiences (CLL)

ELG Extend their vocabulary, exploring the meanings and sounds of new words (CLL)

SS Describe simple features of objects and events (KUW)

ELG Investigate objects and materials by using all their senses as appropriate (KUW)

SS Understand that different media may be combined (CD)

ELG Explore colour, texture, shape, form and space in 2- or 3D (CD)

Extension ideas

1. Link to a topic on the natural environment.
2. Display pictures as a celebration of the season.
3. Provide books on natural materials for the children to look at.
4. Link to other natural play activities (e.g. sand, water, clay, woodworking), explaining the links to the children.

Health and safety

⚠ Careful supervision of all small items
⚠ Ensure that none of the resources are poisonous or harmful to touch
⚠ Avoid sharp or prickly items

Making a honeycomb from hexagons

Resources you will need

- Medium-weight card with hexagon shape pre-drawn or photocopied (see page 87)
- Child-size scissors
- Adult-size scissors
- Yellow paint
- Template for hexagon shape (see p. 87)
- Picture of a honeycomb

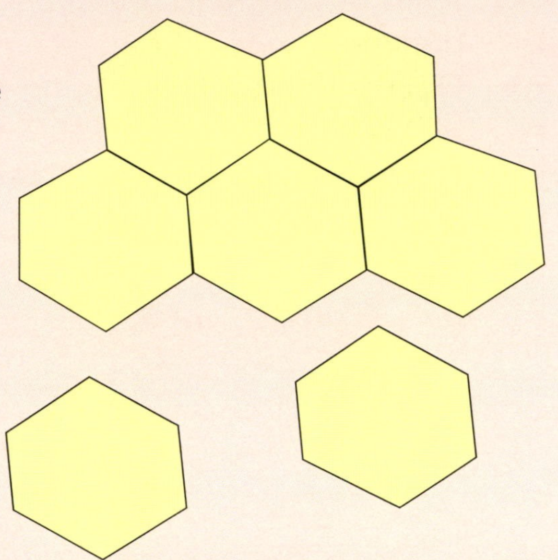

Aim/concept

- To explore the concept of tessellation, using hexagons (six-sided shapes)

Process

- Show the children the template of a hexagon. Ask them what they notice about it (six sides, six points, all even).
- Show them the picture of a honeycomb and help them to make a comparison between the shapes.
- Explain that they are going to make a honeycomb as a group.
- Give each child a piece of (prepared) card and ask them to cut out the hexagon. Adult help may be needed for this.
- Let each child paint their hexagon yellow and leave to dry.
- When all the children have made a yellow hexagon, help them to tessellate them into a honeycomb shape, making reference to the picture of the honeycomb.
- Display the end result prominently, and use for discussion.

Vocabulary/ discussion

- Tessellation – where else is it found, link to bees, counting numbers up to six, bees at work, pollen – nectar – honey

Group size

4 at a time

Links to Foundation Stage Curriculum

SS Respond to simple instructions (CLL)

ELG Sustain attentive listening, responding to what children have heard with relevant comments, questions or actions (CLL)

SS Notice and comment on patterns (KUW)

ELG Look closely at similarities, differences, patterns and change (KUW)

Extension ideas

1. Link to a topic on bees.
2. Bring in beeswax candles for the children to look at.
3. Make beeswax candles using sheets of bees wax tightly rolled up.
4. Eat honey sandwiches (but *only* if there are no children who are allergic to honey or intolerant to gluten).
5. Make hexagon-shaped mats for cups at drinks time.

Health and safety

⚠ Careful supervision of scissor use

ACTIVITY 5

Making wrapping paper

Resources you will need

- White paper (quite thin) (A2 size is ideal)
- A variety of medium-thickness paint (see page 12)
- Shallow dishes for the paint
- A variety of objects with which to print a design

Aim/concept

- To use a printing activity to make a repeated design that may be used for a purpose (e.g. wrapping paper)

Process

- Ask the children to tell you as much as they can about wrapping paper – it's usually colourful, it needs to be large enough to wrap up an object, it often has a distinct pattern and so on.
- Explain that the children are going to design their own wrapping paper, choosing from the range of printing objects you have provided.
- Encourage the children to make additional suggestions for objects to print with.
- Show the children examples of wrapping paper, pointing out the repeated patterns on them. Explain that you want them to try to make a repeated design on their sheet of paper too.
- Show the children how this can be achieved (e.g. printing two circles, one triangle, three stars, two circles, one triangle, three stars).
- Give each child a large sheet of paper and access to paint and printers.
- Talk to the children about their patterns as they work, and encourage them to share their thoughts with each other.

Vocabulary/ discussion

- Shape names, colour names, pattern words such as follows on, repeats, same as, matches, comes next, alongside, parallel

Group size

4–6

Links to Foundation Stage Curriculum

SS Show increasing independence in selecting and carrying out activities (PSE)

ELG Be confident in trying out new activities, initiating ideas and speaking in a familiar group (PSE)

SS Manipulate materials to achieve a planned effect (PD)

ELG Handle tools, objects, construction and malleable materials safely and with increasing control (PD)

SS Work creatively on a large or small scale (CD)

ELG Explore colour, texture, shape, form and space in 2- or 3D (CD)

Extension idea

Link the activity to wrapping up a present to take home (e.g. for Christmas, Easter, Mother's Day).

Health and safety

⚠ Use non-toxic paint

⚠ Supervise

ACTIVITY 6 Making simple pop-up cards

Resources you will need

- Pieces of card
- Child-size scissors
- Adult-size scissors
- Craft lolly sticks
- Pens
- Crayons
- Gummed paper in different colours
- Sticky tape

Aim/concept

- To make a greeting card while exploring simple aspects of technology

Process

- Explain to the children that they are going to make a card for someone of their choice with a pop-up surprise inside.
- Ask the children how they might make something 'move' or 'pop up' within the card.
- Show the children the craft lolly sticks, and explain how these can be attached to whatever they make and slotted through a cut made in the card.
- Encourage the children to decide what their card will be about. You may find it helpful to show them pictures of suitable 'subjects' (e.g. flowers, puppets, people, Father Christmas).
- Give each child a folded piece of card with a slit cut into the underside.
- Let the children decorate the front of their card, and also make the 'subject' for inside.
- Help the children to attach their 'subject' to a lolly stick with sticky tape.
- Let each child demonstrate to the rest of the group how their card pops up.

Vocabulary/ discussion

- Creating, planning, designing, pop up, surprise, movement, cause and effect

Group size

4–6

Links to Foundation Stage Curriculum

SS Demonstrate a sense of pride in own achievement (PSE)

ELG Select and use activities and resources independently (PSE)

SS Use available resources to create props to support role-play (CD)

ELG Use imagination in art and design, music, dance, imaginative and role-play, and stories (CD)

Extension idea

Help the children to make a puppet show using a sturdy box as the puppet theatre, and each child 'working their puppet' along a prepared cut in the side of the box.

Health and safety

⚠ Careful supervision of scissor use

⚠ Always use craft lolly sticks, not from collected sources

ACTIVITY 7

Magnetic fishing

Resources you will need

- A sturdy cardboard box (each side 30–40cm)
- Short lengths of dowelling rod; approximately 50cm would be ideal (garden sticks could be used instead)
- Pieces of string
- Small magnets
- Paper-clips
- Card – orange and red
- Green tissue paper
- Child-size scissors
- Blu-tack

Aim/concept

- To explore magnetic forces by playing a fishing game

Process

- Explain to the children that they are going to make a fish pond and take turns to go fishing.
- Show the children a magnet and ask them what they think it can do.
- Allow time for the children to experience the magnet's properties, perhaps against their shoe buckles or metal buttons.
- Help the children to attach lengths of string to the rods; strong tape should work. Help them to attach the magnets to the string with Blu-tack.
- Encourage the children to cut fish shapes from the orange and red card. Adult help may be needed.
- Help the children to tear up the green tissue paper to make pondweed.
- Let the children put the pondweed into the pond.
- Ask the children if they can think of a way to make the fish be attracted to the magnets. Show them the paper-clips to help guide them.
- Help the children to attach paper-clips to each fish.
- Place all the fish in the pond.
- Who can 'catch' the fish?

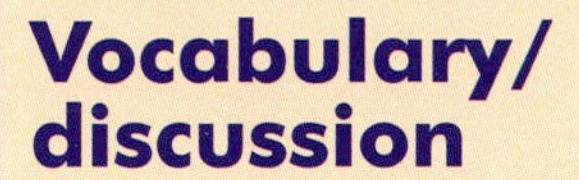

Vocabulary/ discussion

- Magnetic force, attract, repel, catch, how many

Group size

4–6

Links to Foundation Stage Curriculum

SS Talk about what is seen and what is happening (KUW)

ELG Ask questions about why things happen and how things work (KUW)

SS Show curiosity (PSE)

ELG Continue to be interested, excited and motivated to learn (PSE)

SS Manipulate materials and objects by picking up, releasing, arranging, threading and posting them (PD)

ELG Move with control and coordination (PD)

Extension ideas

1. Remove paper-clips from fish – Can they catch them now? Why not?
2. Provide larger magnets and encourage the children to explore the setting to see what else is attracted to magnets.
3. Remove paper-clips from fish and try to make fish move by wafting them along with stiff sheets of card into a chalk circle (pond).
4. Provide a goldfish for the children to watch and care for.

Health and safety

- ⚠ Ensure that magnets are not put in mouths
- ⚠ Careful supervision of scissor use
- ⚠ Careful supervision of how rods are held and handled

ACTIVITY 8

Three-dimensional flying insects

Resources you will need

- Sufficient paper for each child to have two A3-size sheets
- Child-size scissors
- Adult-size scissors (or dual-handle scissors)
- Paint in appropriate colours – yellow, red, black, blue, brown
- Brushes
- Newspaper for padding out the insects
- A large-size stapler
- Black paper
- Fine string or wool

Aim/concept

- To make representations of familiar creatures and to explore the difference between two and three dimensions

Process

- Explain to the children that they are going to make insects that fly to display from the ceiling (or top of the window).
- Ask the children what flying insects they can think of, prompting them to think about colours and patterns. It may be helpful to show the children pictures of different butterflies, moths, bees, ladybirds and so on.
- Give each child two pieces of paper for them to cut into two large insect shapes (adult assistance may be needed). Explain that these are for each side of the body.
- Encourage the children to paint their insects, adding patterns where appropriate.
- Allow time for the insects to dry.
- Help each child to construct their three-dimensional insect by stapling it half-way round and letting the child stuff the shape with newspaper. Staple the rest of the insect carefully.
- Help the children to cut strips of black paper for legs and antennae.
- Discuss with the children where they might see the insects, and at what times during the year.
- Attach string or wool and hang to display.

Vocabulary/ discussion

- Insect names, colours, patterns, shapes, two and three dimensions, flight, discussion of antennae, wings, stings, discussion of when and where the insects may be seen

Group size

4–6

Links to Foundation Stage Curriculum

SS Notice differences between features of the local environment (KUW)

ELG Observe, find out about and identify features in places where the children live and in the natural world (KUW)

SS Make three-dimensional structures (CD)

ELG Explore colour, texture, shape, form and space in 2- or 3D (CD)

Extension ideas

1. Include the newly made 3D insects within display on gardens, insects or flight.
2. Sing rhymes such as 'Ladybird, Ladybird, Fly Away Home'.
3. Provide information books for the children to look at (e.g. *What Lives in the Garden* by John Woodward (Red Kite Books) and *Are You a Bee?* by Judy Allen and Tudor Humphries (Kingfisher Books)).

Health and safety

- ⚠ Careful supervision of scissor use
- ⚠ Adult responsibility to use stapler
- ⚠ Supervision of use of string

Self-portraits

Resources you will need

- An A3 sheet of paper for each child
- Containers of paint, including skin tones for all the children
- Brushes suitable for the children's developmental level
- A safe mirror for each child

Aim/concept

- To help the children focus on the concept of reflections, in particular their own faces, noting and replicating facial features, and any adornments or accessories

Process

- Talk to the children about how they would describe themselves.
- Explore the children's ideas of reflections with them.
- Give each of the children a mirror and ask them to study themselves carefully.
- Ask the children to identify facial features, colours of hair braids and ribbons, spectacles and so on.
- Draw specific attention to difficult aspects of themselves (e.g. eye colour).
- Show the children the range of paint colours and remind them to try to match the colours to what they see in the mirror.
- Talk to the children about skin tones as well as colours in general.
- Supervise the children as they paint their portraits, encouraging, suggesting and valuing their efforts.

Vocabulary/discussion

- Names of facial features (e.g. eyes, nose, mouth, teeth, eyebrows, cheeks, hair, ears)
- Individual characteristics and accessories (e.g. curly, plaited, straight hair; spectacles, hair bands, braiding, ribbons, earrings, clips and slides)
- Discussion of skin tones, cultural identity, familial features

Group size

4–6

Extension ideas

1. Link the activity to a theme on 'Ourselves'.
2. Link to activities on families and let children paint other family members too.
3. Let the children paint portraits of each other.
4. Discuss similarities and differences.
5. Read books such as *That's My Mum* by H. Barkow and D. Brazell (Mantra Publishing).

Links to Foundation Stage Curriculum

SS Demonstrate a sense of pride in own achievement (PSE)

ELG Select and use activities and resources independently (PSE)

SS Engage in activities requiring hand–eye coordination (PD)

ELG Handle tools, objects, construction and malleable materials safely and with increasing control (PD)

SS Choose particular colours to use for a specific purpose (CD)

ELG Explore colour, texture, shape, form and space in 2- or 3D (CD)

Health and safety

⚠ Safety mirrors only should be used

ACTIVITY 10 Model-making with junk

Resources you will need

- A large selection of clean, empty boxes
- Cardboard tubes from kitchen paper rolls or similar
- Pots of glue
- Spatulas
- Sticky tape
- Child-size scissors
- Adult-size scissors
- Stapler (for adult use)
- Pots of thickened paint (see page 12)
- Brushes

Aim/concept

- To enable children to make a construction of their choice from their own ideas and imagination

Process

- Prepare the environment (see page 7).
- Explain to the children that they can make whatever they wish, using the resources provided for them.
- Explain the benefits of allowing a model to dry before painting it and provide a drying space that can be accessed easily by the children.
- Let the children explore and construct freely.
- Support the children's modelling with encouragement and discussion of what they are doing.
- Display the finished models to place value on the children's efforts.

Vocabulary/discussion

- 2- and 3D shape names (e.g. square, rectangle, tube, cube, cuboid, cone)
- Links to size: (e.g. large, largest, small, smallest, tall, short, wide, narrow)
- Positional language (e.g. on top of, behind, in front of)
- Terms such as balanced, sturdy, secure, stable, unstable
- Descriptive names (e.g. exciting, imaginative, pretend)
- Object names (e.g. vehicle, machine, invention)

Group size

4–6

Links to Foundation Stage Curriculum

SS Show willingness to tackle problems, and enjoy self-chosen challenges (PSE)

ELG Select and use activities and resources independently (PSE)

SS Show interest by sustained construction activity or by talking about shapes or arrangements (MD)

ELG Use language (e.g. 'circle' or 'bigger') to describe the shape and size of solid and flat shapes (MD)

SS Manipulate materials to achieve a planned effect (PD)

ELG Handle tools, objects, construction and malleable materials safely and with increasing control (PD)

Extension ideas

1. Link to a topic on robots.
2. Link to a topic on vehicles.
3. Link to a discussion on recycling and waste products.
4. Make a recycling collection box in the setting ready for more 'junk' modelling.
5. Make a 'skyline' of houses and buildings.

Health and safety

- ⚠ Only clean boxes and resources should be used
- ⚠ Toilet roll tubes and medicine boxes must be avoided
- ⚠ Careful supervision of scissor use is needed
- ⚠ Adult use only of stapler

ACTIVITY 11 Printing

Resources you will need

- An apron for each child
- Sheets of paper
- Shallow containers of paint
- Thin layers of sponge (optional) to cover base of containers
- A variety of halved fruits and vegetables: potatoes, peppers, carrots (cut lengthways), large mushrooms, cauliflower florets, apples, pears, star fruits, pomegranates
- A sharp knife – for adult use only

Aim/concept

- To explore the inner (surface) shapes of objects through paint

Process

- Explain to the children what the activity is about.
- Ask the children to name the fruits and vegetables, and to say what they know about each one.
- Talk about the shapes and ask the children to imagine what the shapes might look like when you cut them in half. Encourage the children to use description.
- Cut each item of food into two in turn, showing the two halves to the children and discussing what they see.
- Help the children to make comparisons, noting similarities and differences.
- Encourage the children to make a painting by printing the fruit and vegetable halves in the dishes of paint.
- Display the paintings.

Vocabulary/discussion

- Names of fruits and vegetables
- Colours and shapes of fruits and vegetables
- Words such as halve, divide, split, equal
- Words such as seed, core, stalk, stem, floret, skin, flesh, pip, firm, hard
- Introduce comparative language (e.g. similar to, the same as, compare, resemble)

Group size

4–6

Links to Foundation Stage Curriculum

SS Sort objects by one function (KUW)

ELG Look closely at similarities, differences, patterns and change (KUW)

SS Work creatively on a large or small scale (CD)

ELG Explore colour, texture, shape, form and space in 2- or 3D (CD)

Extension ideas

1. Link to a topic on fruit and vegetables, shopping or healthy eating.
2. Play the game 'I went shopping and in my basket I put . . .', each child repeating what has been said and adding another item as the game moves from person to person.
3. Fold a sheet of paper into four sections (or draw divisions with a pen), then print a different fruit or vegetable in each 'quarter', making an identifying game for others to play.
4. Print using potatoes cut in half with raised shapes cut into them (e.g. square, triangle).
5. Print using sponges cut into simple shapes.
6. Print using cotton reels and plastic lids from jars of coffee, Marmite, peanut butter and mustard.
7. Use the photocopiable sheet on page 80.

Health and safety

⚠ Be aware of any allergies to the fruits and vegetables you use

⚠ Keep the sharp knife safely away from the children

ACTIVITY 12

String painting

Resources you will need

- Sheets of paper, A3 if possible
- An apron for each child
- Shallow dishes of thickened paint (see page 12)
- Lengths of string or thick wool

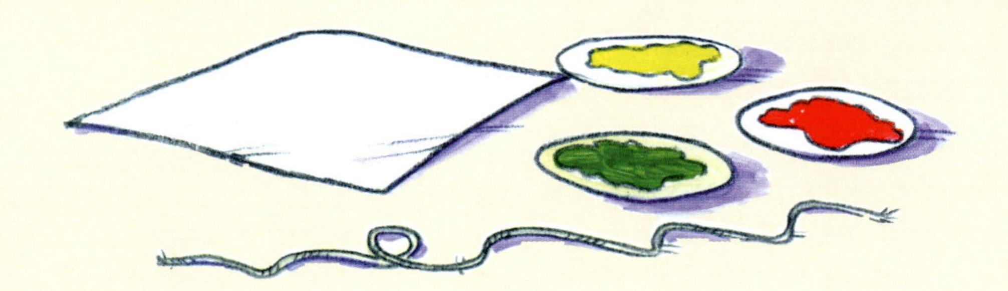

Aim/concept

- To experiment with the effects of paint-soaked string pulled through folded sheets of paper

Process

- Explain to the children that you are going to try to make a pattern by pulling paint-soaked string through folded sheets of paper.
- Show the children how to fold a sheet of paper in half.
- Explain that they need to take a length of string and dip it into a dish of paint.
- Show the children how to place the wet string on one side of the paper with one end close to the bottom.
- Help the children to fold their paper in half.
- Show the children how to press down with one hand on to the folded paper.
- Explain that using the other hand they will need to pull the string slowly through the folded paper.
- Everyone looks to see the pattern they have made.
- Encourage the children to add another colour, building up the patterns each time they add another string to the design.

Vocabulary/ discussion

- Discuss terms such as fold, equal, matching, pull, slither, press, hold
- Use colour names and colour blends
- Discuss resulting patterns and what shapes can be seen in them

Group size

4–6

Links to Foundation Stage Curriculum

SS Manipulate materials and objects by picking up, releasing, arranging, threading and posting them (PD)

ELG Move with control and coordination (PD)

SS Manipulate materials to achieve a planned effect (PD)

ELG Handle tools, objects, construction and malleable materials safely and with increasing control (PD)

SS Experiment to create different textures (CD)

ELG Explore colour, texture, shape, form and space in 2- or 3D (CD)

Extension ideas

Use netting from vegetable and nut bags in the same way.

Health and safety

⚠ Ensure string is not put around the children's necks

ACTIVITY 13 Bubble painting

Resources you will need

- Paper that will absorb paint (sugar paper is ideal)
- Pots of thin paint
- A drinking straw for each child

Aim/concept

- To make changes to paint for a purpose

Process

- Explore with the children the difference between sucking and blowing.
- Get each child to show you how they can blow through a straw.
- Ask the children why it is important to each have their own straw.
- Ask the children what might happen if they blow through their straw into the paint.
- Let them try, encouraging them to blow slowly, but hard.
- Talk about the resulting bubbles, asking the children how they might 'capture' the bubbles for a picture.
- Demonstrate how to place paper carefully over the bubbles to 'capture' the image.
- Encourage the children to make a bubble picture using as many colours as they wish.

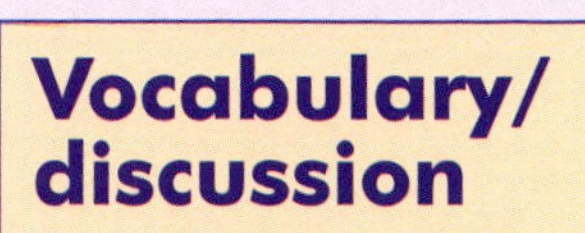

Vocabulary/discussion

- Bubbles, circles, patterns
- Pop, burst, disperse
- Image, record, capture, print
- Discuss with the children where the bubbles go to, what they are made from, why they are so fragile and so on
- Hygiene issues, cross-infection

Group size

4–6

Links to Foundation Stage Curriculum

SS Talk about what is seen and what is happening (KUW)

ELG Ask questions about why things happen and how things work (KUW)

SS Show awareness of a range of healthy practices with regard to eating, sleeping and hygiene (PD)

ELG Recognise the importance of keeping healthy and those things which contribute to this (PD)

SS Experiment to create different textures (CD)

ELG Explore colour, texture, shape, form and space in 2- or 3D (CD)

Extension ideas

1. Include within a topic on shapes (circles).
2. Link to discussions on air.
3. Follow up with blowing bubbles outside.
4. Make your own bubble mixture with water and washing-up liquid.

Health and safety

⚠ Ensure that all children can blow, to ensure that no paint is accidentally sucked up the straws

⚠ Ensure each child has their own straw

Butterfly prints

Resources you will need

- Sheets of paper
- Pots of paint – various colours
- Brushes

Aim/concept

- To replicate a painted image

Process

- Talk to the children about butterflies. What do they notice about them?
- If necessary, draw their attention to how the wings are often similar.
- Discuss ways of making images match.
- Where have the children seen matching images?
- Explain how the children can replicate their painting by folding the paper in half afterwards while the paint is still wet.
- Let each child make a fold in their sheet of paper.
- Encourage the children to paint a design on one 'half' of the folded sheet of paper.
- Encourage the children to fold over their sheets of paper and press down to make the replicated image.
- What happens if they paint a design on both 'halves' of the paper?

Vocabulary/discussion

- Use terms such as fold, half, reproduce, similar, match, same as, flatten, press down, smooth out
- Talk about matching images

Group size

4–6

Links to Foundation Stage Curriculum

- SS Show awareness of symmetry (MD)
- ELG Talk about, recognise and re-create simple patterns (MD)
- SS Notice and comment on patterns (KUW)
- ELG Look closely at similarities, difference, patterns and change (KUW)

Extension ideas

1. Link to activities (butterflies, insects, gardens and so on).
2. Let the children reproduce images using a mirror.
3. Play pairs games, matching pictures from memory.
4. Read stories such as *The Very Hungry Caterpillar* by Eric Carle (Hamish Hamilton).

Health and safety

⚠ No specific issues to take into consideration

ACTIVITY 15 Sewing card calendars

Resources you will need

- Pieces of stiff card – A5 is ideal
- A hole puncher
- A skewer (optional)
- A selection of calendars, both commercially and individually made
- A selection of clear pictures (optional)
- PVA glue
- Crayons or felt-tip pens (optional)
- A large bodkin (blunt needle) for each child
- Wool in various colours
- Small individual calendars
- Narrow ribbon
- Scissors – child size
- Scissors – Adult size
- Sticky tape

Aim/concept

- To use manipulative dexterity to design and make a calendar

Process

- Talk to the children about how we use calendars to keep note of the date and so on.
- Show them your examples.
- Explain that they are going to make a calendar, and sew around the edges to make it extra-special.
- Give each child a piece of card.
- Let the children either choose a picture to stick on to the card, or to draw a picture themselves.
- Using a hole puncher, demonstrate how holes can be made around the edges of the card for sewing. Explain the importance of punching the holes as far from the edge of the card as possible. You may need to do this for some children.
- Thread a length of wool for each child on to a bodkin, ensuring that a large knot is tied at the end.

- Demonstrate how to sew, pulling all the wool through the hole at each 'stitch'.
- Instead (or as well), make holes around the picture or drawing on the card with the skewer (adult activity only). Let the children sew the picture shape.
- When the sewing has been completed, let each child cut a short length of ribbon (about the length of their piece of card).
- Help the children to attach a loop to the top of the card with sticky tape.
- Help the children to attach the calendar to the bottom of the card with sticky tape.

Vocabulary/discussion

- Vocabulary linked to dates: seasons, birthdays, festivals and so on
- Terms such as sew, stitch, join, design, decorate, thread, bodkin, needle
- Positional language (e.g. in, out, behind, next, the following)
- Colours of wool used

Links to Foundation Stage Curriculum

SS Observe and use positional language (MD)
ELG Use everyday words to describe position (MD)
SS Begin to try out a range of tools and techniques safely (KUW)
ELG Select the tools and techniques needed to shape, assemble and join the materials (KUW)
SS Understand that equipment and tools have to be used safely (PD)
SS Manipulate materials to achieve a planned effect (PD)
ELG Handle tools, objects, construction and malleable materials safely and with increasing control (PD)

Group size

2–4

Extension ideas

1. Decorate a greetings card for a special occasion (e.g Mother's Day, Easter, Divali).
2. Make a decorated photograph frame to give as a present.

Health and safety

- Careful supervision of scissor use
- Adults only to use skewer
- Care to be taken with bodkins, explaining to the children that they must not put them near their own or anyone else's eyes

Wax paintings

Resources you will need

- Sheets of absorbent paper (sugar paper is ideal)
- Candles (or good-quality wax crayons)
- Pots of thin paint
- Brushes

Aim/concept

- To explore the properties of paint on wax

Process

- Encourage the children to draw with candles on the sugar paper. Wax crayons may be used, but are not usually as successful.
- Ask the children to touch the wax and describe how it feels.
- Explain that the wax does something special, and ask the children if they know what it might be.
- Encourage the children to paint all over their sheet of paper with the thin paint.
- Discuss with them what they see (the wax does not absorb the paint).

Vocabulary/ discussion

- Introduce terms such as image, repel, wash over
- Encourage descriptive terms (of the wax) (e.g. smooth, sticky, tacky)
- What does it feel like? Smell like?

Group size

4–6

Links to Foundation Stage Curriculum

SS Adopt a positive approach to new experiences (PSE)

ELG Continue to be interested, excited and motivated to learn (PSE)

SS Talk about what is seen and what is happening (KUW)

ELG Look closely at similarities, differences, patterns and change (KUW)

SS Further explore an experience using a range of senses (CD)

ELG Respond in a variety of ways to what is seen, heard, smelled, touched and felt (CD)

Extension ideas

1. Use candles on white paper to make 'magic' writing.
2. Link to a topic that involves finding out about bees.

Health and safety

⚠ Ensure no child puts wax into their mouth

⚠ If beeswax is used, be aware of allergies

Hand printing

Resources you will need

- Sheets of paper – A3 is ideal
- Large, shallow dishes of paint – slightly thickened (see page 12)
- Either a waterproof covering or plenty of newspaper for the table (see page 7)
- An apron for each child
- A large bowl of warm, soapy water
- Towel or paper towels

Aim/concept

- To explore the feel of paint and to print using hands

Process

- Prepare the environment carefully, covering the table to be used with the waterproof sheet or newspaper. Ensure that no other activity will be affected by the potential 'mess' of this one.
- Help the children to put on aprons to protect their clothes.
- Encourage the children to handle the paint, and to describe what they feel.
- You may wish to use specially prepared finger paints (see page 14).
- When the children have explored the paint as much as they wish, encourage them to make hand prints on the paper.

Vocabulary/discussion

- Vocabulary linked to colour and paint texture
- Counting up to five (fingers)
- Mathematical comparisons (e.g. smaller than, larger than, the same size as)

Group size

4

Extension ideas

1. Use hand prints to make feathered displays (e.g. an owl, or a swan, or spring chicks).
2. Use hand prints to make a rainbow.
3. Cut round the hand prints and stick the palms down for a more 'feathery' effect.
4. Use hand printing to form a border for a display on friendship.
5. Make friendship cards for the children to give to each other.

Links to Foundation Stage Curriculum

SS Have a positive approach to new experiences (PSE)

ELG Continue to be interested, excited and motivated to learn (PSE)

SS Begin to describe the texture of things (CD)

ELG Explore colour, texture, shape, form and space in 2- or 3D (CD)

Health and safety

⚠ Ensure paint from hands does not reach mouths

⚠ Supervise hand-washing

⚠ Refresh the bowl of water for hand-washing regularly

Foot printing

Resources you will need

- Ideally, two adults would work together during this activity
- A roll of lining paper or plain wallpaper
- Large, shallow dishes of paint – slightly thickened (see page 12)
- A waterproof covering and plenty of newspaper for the floor
- A large bowl of warm, soapy water
- Towel or paper towels

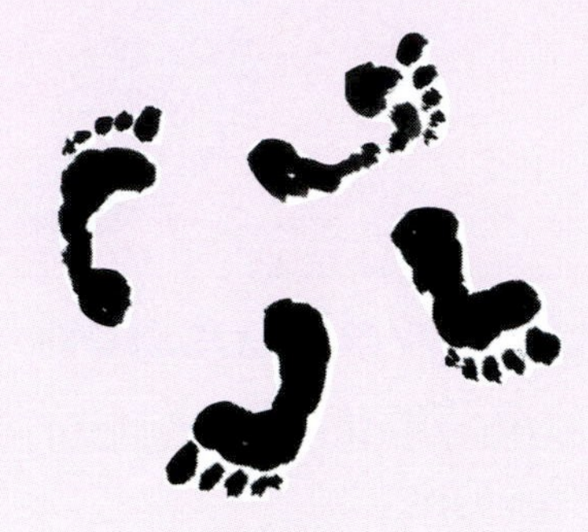

Aim/concept

- To explore paint with our feet, and making foot prints

Process

- Prepare the environment carefully, covering the floor with the waterproof sheet and then the newspaper. Ensure that no other activity will be affected by the potential 'mess' of this one.
- Help the children to roll up their trousers and take off their socks to protect their clothes.
- Explain to the children that they are going to need to stand in the paint.
- Discuss with the children the importance of waiting patiently and taking turns.
- Explain to the children that they can print with their feet by stepping from the dishes of paint and walking along the roll of paper, slowly – no running.
- Hold each child's hand as they step into the dishes of paint, since paint can be slippery.
- Encourage the children to describe how it feels.
- When the children have explored the paint with their feet and toes, encourage them to walk along the roll of paper making foot prints.
- Help each child to wash their feet thoroughly and dry them on the towels.

Vocabulary/discussion

- Vocabulary linked to colour and paint texture
- Mathematical comparisons (e.g. smaller than, larger than, longest, shortest, the same size as and so on)
- Positional language (e.g. in front of, behind, next to, forwards, backwards, sideways)

Group size

2–4

Links to Foundation Stage Curriculum

SS Have an awareness of the boundaries set and behavioural expectations within the setting (PSE)

ELG Understand what is right, what is wrong, and why (PSE)

SS Observe and use positional language (MD)

ELG Use everyday words to describe position (MD)

SS Manage the body to create intended movements (PD)

ELG Move with control and co-ordination (MD)

Extension idea

Cut out foot prints and make them into stepping stones by mounting them on to sheets of cardboard. Make a trail around the setting for children to follow.

Health and safety

- ⚠ Ensure that the children wait their turn patiently and calmly
- ⚠ Hold children securely when they are standing in the dishes of paint
- ⚠ Enforce a 'No running' rule
- ⚠ Supervise the washing of children's feet
- ⚠ Refresh the bowl of water for feet-washing regularly
- ⚠ Ensure no child walks around the setting with wet feet
- ⚠ Mop up any spills to avoid accidents

ACTIVITY 19 Using appliqué to make a mural

Resources you will need

- A large piece of hessian, or similar material
- Bodkins
- Balls of wool
- Pieces of material of differing textures and colours
- PVA glue
- Spatulas
- Scissors – child size
- Scissors – adult size
- Stapler – for adult use

Aim/concept

- To work together to produce a large picture using a variety of skills and media

Process

- This activity will often take more than one 'session' to complete.
- Agree with the children in advance of the activity what the picture will be about. This will usually be linked with a current topic.
- Encourage the children to bring in suitable pieces of material (e.g. wool) to be included.
- Help the children to plan what they will each contribute and where it will be placed. As the adult, you will need to help them to plan scale and position, perhaps with a rough sketch on a large sheet of paper (e.g. if making a road scene, show them how houses need to be at the side of the road and cars along the middle). Agree where trees, traffic-lights and so on might go.
- It may be helpful to pencil some guidelines on to the hessian 'background'.
- Help each child to contribute an item of their choice to the picture.
- You may need to help with cutting, or holding material or wool steady for them.
- Encourage the children to sew or glue items on to the hessian.
- Encourage the children to talk about the materials they are using.
- Build the picture up gradually.
- Display the finished mural on the wall.

Vocabulary/discussion

- Topical words and phrases dependent on the mural design chosen by the children
- Terms such as mural, design, plan, outline, position, attach, join, add to, contribute, develop, build up, texture
- Discuss the scene with the children. What do they think is happening?

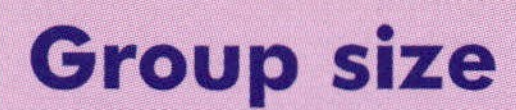

Group size

2

Links to Foundation Stage Curriculum

SS Display high levels of involvement in activities (PSE)

ELG Be confident to try new activities, initiate ideas and speak in a familiar group (PSE)

SS Have emerging self-confidence to speak to others about wants and interests (CLL)

ELG Interact with others, negotiating plans and activities and taking turns in conversations (CLL)

SS Manipulate materials to achieve a planned effect (PD)

ELG Handle tools, objects, construction and malleable materials safely and with increasing control (PD)

Extension ideas

1. Encourage the children to tell each other about what they have contributed to the mural, perhaps during a group time session.
2. Use a group time session to encourage the children to develop a story about their mural – What's happening?, Who might live there? What might be growing? and so on.

Health and safety

⚠ Careful supervision of scissor use

⚠ Care to be taken with bodkins, explaining to the children that they must not put them near their own or anyone else's eyes

⚠ Adult only to use stapler

ACTIVITY 20 Finger painting

Resources you will need

- A clear surface away from other activities. See Preparing the environment (page 7).
- An apron for each child
- Arm bands (particularly useful for younger children)
- Containers of specially prepared paint (see page 14)
- Large sheets of paper – A3 is ideal (optional)
- Hand-washing facilities near to hand

Aim/concept

- To experience the feel of paint, without the restriction of brushes or other implements

Process

- Prepare the paint so that it is no longer runny.
- Or – make the paint with the children (see recipes on pages 14–15).
- Ensure that the children's clothes are well covered.
- Ensure that each child has plenty of room.
- Let each child tip out a generous amount of paint on to the work surface.
- Encourage the children to explore with their hands and fingers.
- Talk with the children about what they are experiencing.
- If desired, help the children take a print of their 'designs' by placing a sheet of paper over the paint and pressing down firmly.
- Do not hurry them to the printing stage. Let them explore for as long as possible.

Vocabulary/discussion

- Use terms such as smooth, glide, splosh, swish, swirl, smooth, soft, frothy, creamy, pattern, change

Group size

2–4

Links to Foundation Stage Curriculum

SS Explore malleable materials by patting, stroking, poking, squeezing, pinching and twisting them (PD)

ELG Handle tools, objects, construction and malleable materials safely and with increasing control (PD)

SS Begin to describe the texture of things (CD)

ELG Explore colour, texture, shape, form and space in 2- or 3D (CD)

Extension ideas

1. Use prints for a background display.
2. Let the children make hand prints.
3. Try using mud!
4. Introduce the children to gloop.

Health and safety

⚠ Be aware of spillages

⚠ Children with skin allergies may need to wear disposable gloves

ACTIVITY 21 Using patchwork designs

Resources you will need

- Sheets of paper or squares of old sheeting
- Paper divided into squares – optional (see photocopiable page 83)
- Pieces of material, wallpaper, coloured paper and so on for cutting up
- A tray of cut-up squares ready prepared for younger children to use
- Child-size scissors
- Adult-size scissors
- Pots of PVA glue
- Spatulas
- Pots of paint in a variety of colours
- Paintbrushes

Aim/concept

- To introduce the concept of tessellation

Process

- Explain to the children what tessellation is and ask them to think about where they may have seen it.
- Explain what they are going to be doing with their tessellating (e.g. making a large wall display).
- Encourage the children to select paper, materials and so on to make their design.
- Show them how to cut out squares – you may need to do this for them, or offer them choices from those already prepared.
- Encourage them to tessellate, covering either the materials, paper or prepared sheets. You may need to help younger children as they try to match the edges together.
- Display the results to match a large patchwork wall covering.

Vocabulary/discussion

- Introduce terms such as tessellate, match, adjoining, next to, square, shape
- Talk about lining squares up, laying alongside, setting out rows
- Count the squares with the children, and talk about their colours and designs

Group size

4–6

Links to Foundation Stage Curriculum

SS Match some shapes by recognising similarities and orientation (MD)

ELG Talk about, recognise and re-create simple patterns (MD)

SS Manipulate materials to achieve a planned effect (PD)

ELG Handle tools, objects, construction and malleable materials safely and with increasing control (PD)

SS Work creatively on a large or small scale (CD)

ELG Explore colour, texture, shape, form and space in 2- or 3D (CD)

Extension ideas

1. Make a patchwork quilt on a wall display of a bed.
2. Read the story *The Patchwork Cat* by Nicola Bayley and William Mayne (Picture Puffins).
3. Read the story *Elmer* by David McKee (Red Fox).
4. Make a display of Elmer elephants using patchwork designs.

Health and safety

⚠ Careful supervision of scissor use

ACTIVITY 22 Making playdough with the children

Resources you will need

- An apron for each child
- A clean, washable surface
- A large mixing bowl
- Flour – type dependent on recipe being used (see pages 21–3)
- Salt (if recipe requires it)
- A large jug of water
- Wooden spoons

Aim/concept

- To explore the effects of combining ingredients for a purpose

Process

- If practical, allow the children to collect the ingredients from the store cupboard.
- Ensure that all the children have washed their hands well.
- Wipe the table with an antibacterial cleaner.
- Explain to the children what type of dough they are going to make – ideally let them choose.
- Talk through the recipe card for making dough (see page 85).
- Let the children take turns to add the ingredients.
- Let each child take a turn in mixing the dough.
- Give each child a lump of the dough to knead until smooth.
- You may need to combine all the dough together once again to complete the kneading.
- The dough is ready to use.
- Encourage the children to handle the dough directly before introducing tools and other 'dough' implements.

Vocabulary/discussion

- Discuss the actions taking place: combine, mix, knead, pull, poke, roll, twist and so on
- Depending on the type of dough being used, talk to the children about its properties, using vocabulary such as stretchy, pliable, elastic, model, mass, break apart, lump, impression

Group size

4–6

Links to Foundation Stage Curriculum

SS Display high levels of involvement in activities (PSE)

ELG Continue to be interested, excited and motivated to learn (PSE)

SS Build up vocabulary that reflects the breadth of the children's experiences (CLL)

ELG Extend their vocabulary, exploring the meanings and sounds of new words (CLL)

SS Explore malleable materials by patting, poking, squeezing, pinching and twisting them (PD)

ELG Handle tools, objects, construction and malleable materials safely and with increasing control (PD)

Extension ideas

1. Bake dough 'items' made by the children, to be painted and varnished as a later activity.
2. Help the children to make pots or 'food' for the role-play area.
3. Try putting the playdough near to the role-play area (with a cooker in it). This promotes some inspiring 'cooking' play.

Health and safety

- Supervised hand-washing
- Activity surface to be thoroughly cleaned before use
- Hands to be kept away from mouths and faces

ACTIVITY 23 Weaving

Resources you will need

- Two pieces of wooden baton (approximately 40cm long)
- A ball of string or strong wool
- Material cut into strips (approximately 20cm wider than the loom)

Aim/concept

- To build on manipulative dexterity skills

Process

- Talk to the children about weaving and ask them to think of things that have been woven. Draw their attention to their clothes, and other appropriate items around the setting.
- Explain to the children that they are going to weave a panel of material together and show them the items needed to make the 'loom'.
- If possible, have holes already drilled along each piece of wooden baton.
- Thread string in a zigzag effect, holding the two batons apart at a distance of 40 to 50cm to make a 'loom'. Older children may be able to help with this process.
- Alternatively, secure one end of the string and simply wind it from end to end along the batons to achieve a 'loom' effect, securing the other end as well.
- Encourage the children to select strips of material to weave with.
- Show them how to weave in and out of the strings on the loom, leaving excess material loose at the sides.
- When the woven panel is complete, attach a string for hanging it.
- Display panel on the wall of the setting.

Vocabulary/discussion

- Use terms such as in, out, over, under, behind, in front, weave, create

Group size

2

Links to Foundation Stage Curriculum

SS Use simple tools and techniques competently and appropriately (KUW)

ELG Select the tools and techniques children need to shape, assemble and join materials they are using (KUW)

SS Manipulate materials to achieve a planned effect (PD)

ELG Handle tools, objects, construction and malleable materials safely and with increasing control (PD)

SS Use ideas involving fitting, overlapping, in and out, enclosure, grids and sun-like shapes (CD)

ELG Explore colour, texture, shape, form and space in 2- or 3D (CD)

Extension ideas

1. Weave with paper strips to make mats.
2. Tie four plastic straws together and help each child to make a mini-loom.
3. Make decorations for a festival or party by weaving paper strips over and over (using wedges cut from packs of two different coloured crepe papers).

Health and safety

⚠ Ensure wooden baton is free of splinters

⚠ Supervise use of long lengths of string

ACTIVITY 24

Mixing paint

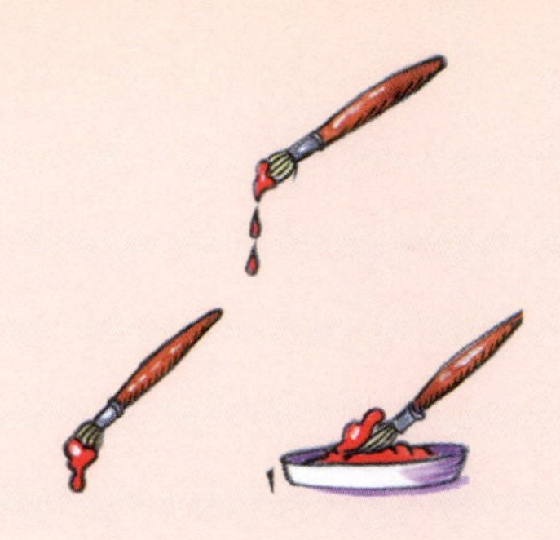

Resources you will need

- An apron for each child
- Arm bands for younger children
- Dishes of powder paint in a variety of colours
- Dishes of cornflour
- Dishes of sand
- Dishes of sawdust
- Dishes of powder paste (still in powder form)
- Dishes of soap flakes
- A bottle of washing-up liquid
- A jug of whipped-up washing-up liquid
- A jug of water
- Empty margarine tubs
- Metal spoons
- Hand-washing facilities nearby

Aim/concept

- To encourage experimentation with different mixtures

Process

- Explain to the children that they are going to make their own paints.
- Talk through the various ingredients that are available to them.
- Encourage them to select an empty tub and gradually combine different ingredients together.
- Encourage the children to talk to each other about the changes they are seeing in the mixture, explaining what ingredients they have added.
- Provide opportunities for them to paint with their own 'paints', either on easels or at a different table.
- Help them to make comparisons between different outcomes.

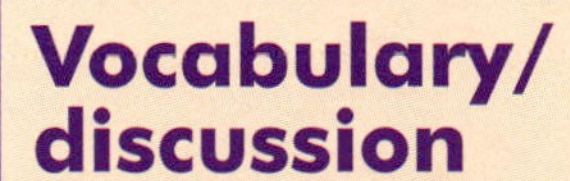

Vocabulary/ discussion

- According to each child's paint mixture, introduce vocabulary such as mix, pour, thicken, change, frothy, gritty, stir
- Ask children how the paint feels on their fingers, and talk about its texture, colour, smell and visual appeal

Group size

2–4

Links to Foundation Stage Curriculum

SS Show increasing independence in selecting and carrying out activities (PSE)

ELG Be confident to try new activities, initiate ideas and speak in a familiar group (PSE)

SS Describe simple features of objects and events (KUW)

ELG Investigate objects and materials by using all senses as appropriate (KUW)

SS Further explore an experience using a range of senses (CD)

ELG Respond in a variety of ways to what the children see, hear, smell, touch and feel (CD)

Extension ideas

1. Link to topic on science or change.
2. Display different types of end result clearly labelled, with examples of the ingredients also displayed.

Health and safety

- ⚠ Ensure the children are well covered
- ⚠ Supervise carefully to minimise spills
- ⚠ Thorough hand-washing when activity is finished

Name ______________________________ **Date** ______________

© Sandy Green (2004) *Creativity*, published by David Fulton Publishers Ltd.

Name ______________________ **Date** ______________

© Sandy Green (2004) *Creativity*, published by David Fulton Publishers Ltd.

red

Name ______________________ **Date** ____________

© Sandy Green (2004) *Creativity*, published by David Fulton Publishers Ltd.

Name ______________________ **Date** ____________

© Sandy Green (2004) *Creativity*, published by David Fulton Publishers Ltd.

Which potato made which prints?

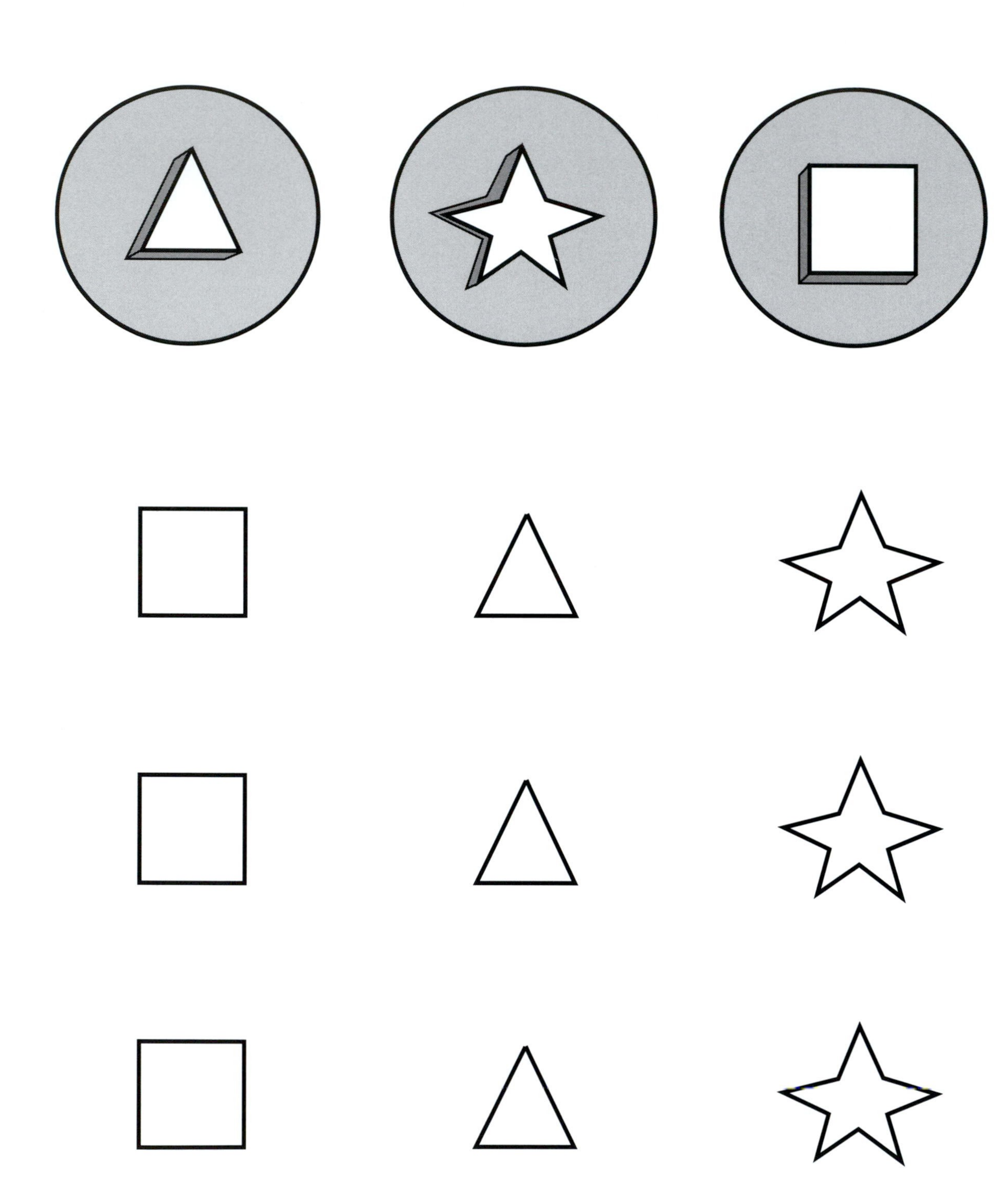

Name ______________________________ **Date** ______________

© Sandy Green (2004) *Creativity*, published by David Fulton Publishers Ltd.

Can you complete the pictures?

Name ______________________________ **Date** ______________

© Sandy Green (2004) *Creativity*, published by David Fulton Publishers Ltd.

Can you design a Mehndi pattern on this hand?

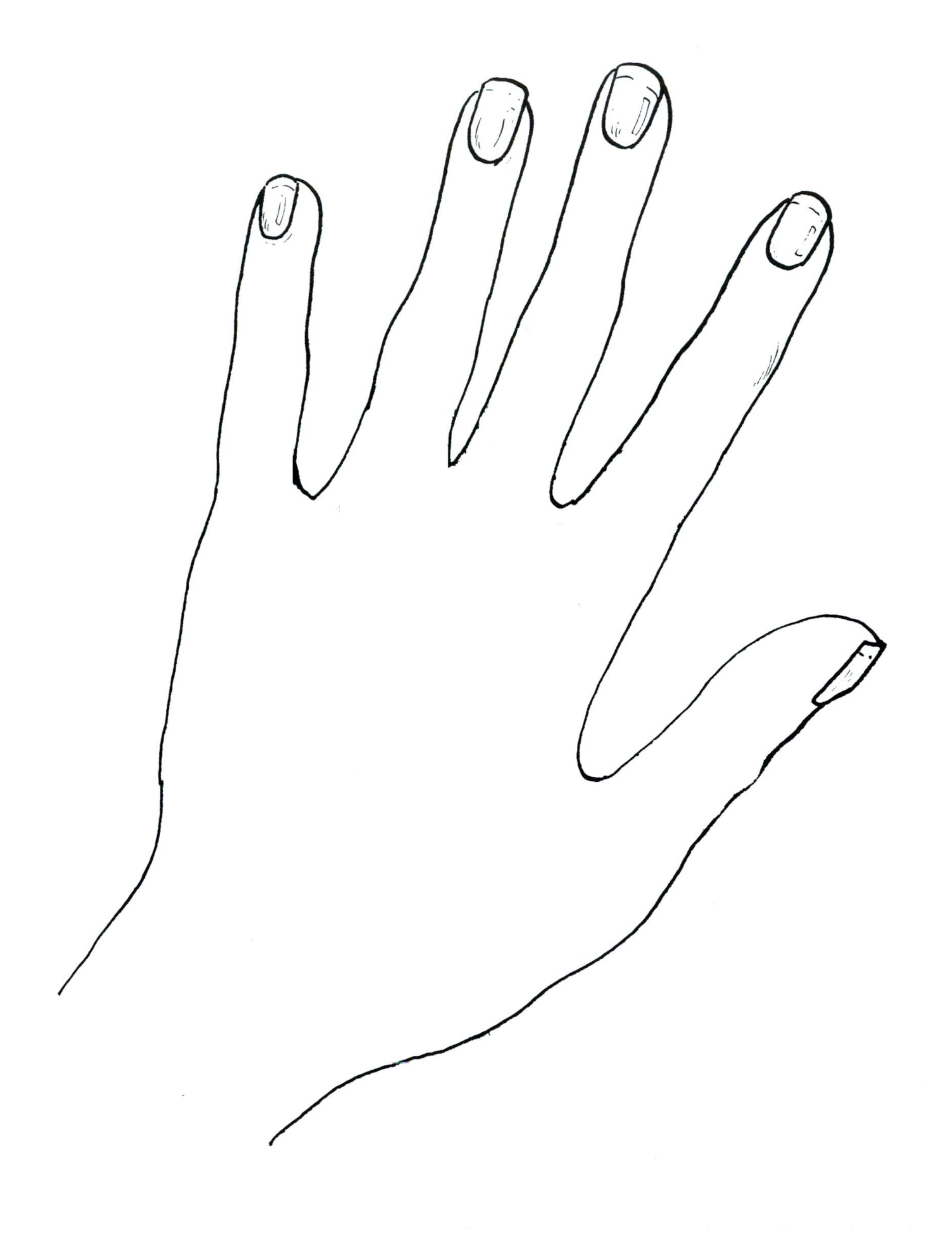

Name ______________________________ **Date** ______________

© Sandy Green (2004) *Creativity*, published by David Fulton Publishers Ltd.

Make your own patchwork squares

Name ______________________ **Date** ______________

© Sandy Green (2004) *Creativity*, published by David Fulton Publishers Ltd.

Photocopy and cut out a number of these sheets

Can you link up these patterns?

Name ______________________ **Date** ______________

© Sandy Green (2004) *Creativity*, published by David Fulton Publishers Ltd.

Playdough recipe card

Ingredients

Bag of flour
Container of salt
Jug of water
Bowl
Wooden spoons

Apron for each child
A clean, washable surface
A large mixing bowl
Wooden spoons

Method

1. Collect the ingredients together.
2. Everyone to wash their hands well.
3. Wipe the table with an antibacterial cleaner.
4. Weigh the ingredients according to the chosen recipe.
5. Take turns to add the ingredients to the mixing bowl.
6. Mix the dough well.
7. Each child has a lump of the dough to knead until smooth.
8. You may need to combine all the dough together once again to complete the kneading.

Name ______________________________ **Date** ________________

© Sandy Green (2004) *Creativity*, published by David Fulton Publishers Ltd.

What made each pattern?

What do you think made each of these patterns?
Draw a line from each object to the correct pattern.

Name ______________________________ **Date** ______________

© Sandy Green (2004) *Creativity*, published by David Fulton Publishers Ltd.

Template of a hexagon

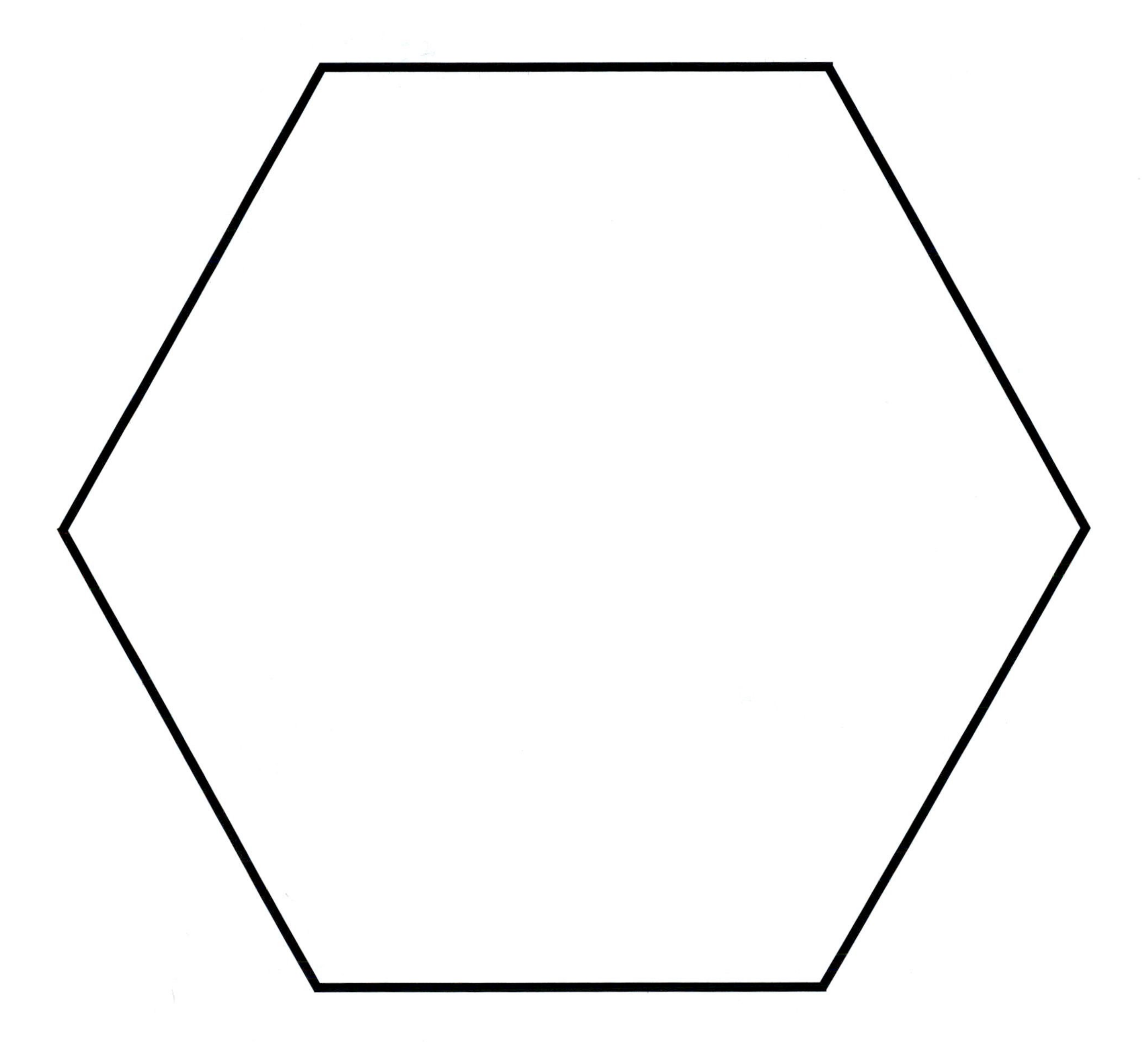

Name ______________________________ **Date** ______________

© Sandy Green (2004) *Creativity*, published by David Fulton Publishers Ltd.

7060